Soothing Piano Worship

20 PEACEFUL SACRED SONGS FOR PIANO

Arranged by Phillip Keveren

— PIANO LEVEL —
INTERMEDIATE TO ADVANCED

ISBN 978-1-70511-394-3

HAL•LEONARD®

For all works contained herein:
Unauthorized copying, arranging, adapting, recording, internet posting, public performance,
or other distribution of the music in this publication is an infringement of copyright.
Infringers are liable under the law.

Visit Hal Leonard Online at
www.halleonard.com

Visit Phillip at
www.phillipkeveren.com

World headquarters, contact:
Hal Leonard
7777 West Bluemound Road
Milwaukee, WI 53213
Email: info@halleonard.com

In Europe, contact:
Hal Leonard Europe Limited
1 Red Place
London, W1K 6PL
Email: info@halleonardeurope.com

In Australia, contact:
Hal Leonard Australia Pty. Ltd.
4 Lentara Court
Cheltenham, Victoria, 3192 Australia
Email: info@halleonard.com.au

PREFACE

These arrangements were crafted to be tranquil, peaceful reflections of the original worship songs. As you interpret the settings, keep the dynamics subdued and the *tempi* spacious. Allow the piano to ring, using the damper pedal generously.

Sincerely,

BIOGRAPHY

Phillip Keveren, a multi-talented keyboard artist and composer, writes original works in a variety of genres from piano solo to symphonic orchestra. He gives frequent concerts and workshops for teachers and their students in the United States, Canada, Europe, and Asia. Mr. Keveren holds a B.M. in composition from California State University Northridge and a M.M. in composition from the University of Southern California.

CONTENTS

AMAZING GRACE
(My Chains Are Gone)

Words by JOHN NEWTON
Traditional American Melody
Additional Words and Music by CHRIS TOMLIN
and LOUIE GIGLIO
Arranged by Phillip Keveren

Gently singing ♩ = c. 72

© 2006 worshiptogether.com Songs (ASCAP), sixsteps Music (ASCAP) and VAMOS PUBLISHING (ASCAP)
This arrangement © 2022 worshiptogether.com Songs (ASCAP), sixsteps Music (ASCAP) and VAMOS PUBLISHING (ASCAP)
Admin. at CAPITOLCMGPUBLISHING.COM
All Rights Reserved   Used by Permission

BUILD MY LIFE

Words and Music by MATT REDMAN,
PAT BARRETT, BRETT YOUNKER,
KARL MARTIN and KIRBY KAPLE
Arranged by Phillip Keveren

Gently ♩ = c. 69

With pedal

© 2016 THANKYOU MUSIC (PRS), HOUSEFIRES SOUNDS (ASCAP), worshiptogether.com Songs (ASCAP), sixsteps Music (ASCAP),
SAID AND DONE MUSIC (ASCAP), CAPITOL CMG GENESIS (ASCAP), SENTRIC MUSIC LIMITED o/b/o ARKYARD MUSIC SERVICES LIMITED and BETHEL MUSIC PUBLISHING
This arrangement © 2022 THANKYOU MUSIC (PRS), HOUSEFIRES SOUNDS (ASCAP), worshiptogether.com Songs (ASCAP), sixsteps Music (ASCAP),
SAID AND DONE MUSIC (ASCAP), CAPITOL CMG GENESIS (ASCAP), SENTRIC MUSIC LIMITED o/b/o ARKYARD MUSIC SERVICES LIMITED and BETHEL MUSIC PUBLISHING
THANKYOU MUSIC Admin. Worldwide at CAPITOLCMGPUBLISHING.COM excluding Europe which is Admin. by INTEGRITY MUSIC, a part of the DAVID C COOK family.
SONGS@INTEGRITYMUSIC.COM
HOUSEFIRES SOUNDS, worshiptogether.com Songs, sixsteps Music, SAID AND DONE MUSIC and CAPITOL CMG GENESIS Admin. at CAPITOLCMGPUBLISHING.COM
All Rights Reserved   Used by Permission

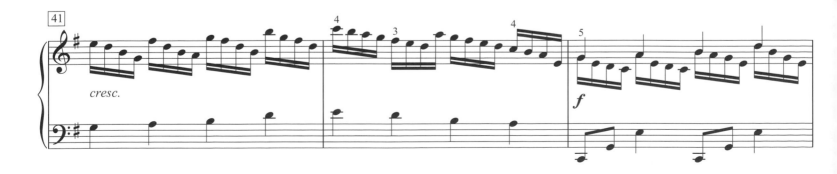

CORNERSTONE

Words and Music by JONAS MYRIN,
REUBEN MORGAN, ERIC LILJERO
and EDWARD MOTE
Arranged by Phillip Keveren

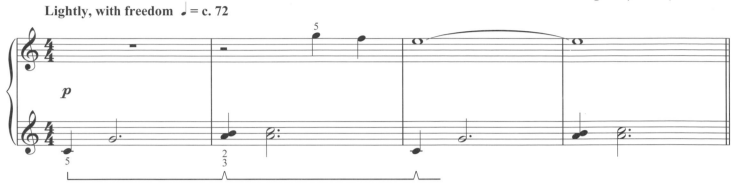

© 2012 HILLSONG MUSIC PUBLISHING (APRA)
This arrangement © 2022 HILLSONG MUSIC PUBLISHING (APRA)
Admin. in the United States and Canada at CAPITOLCMGPUBLISHING.COM
All Rights Reserved   Used by Permission

GLORIOUS DAY

Words and Music by SEAN CURRAN,
KRISTIAN STANFILL, JASON INGRAM
and JONATHAN SMITH
Arranged by Phillip Keveren

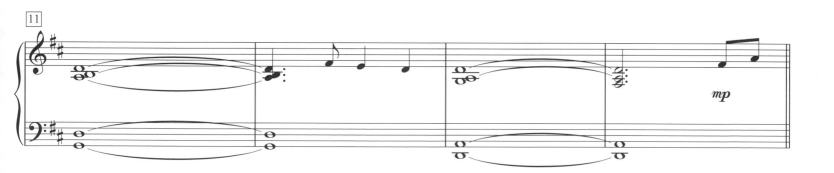

© 2017 SOUNDS OF JERICHO (BMI), KRISTIAN STANFILL PUBLISHING DESIGNEE (NS), worshiptogether.com Songs (ASCAP), WORSHIP TOGETHER MUSIC (BMI),
sixsteps Music (ASCAP), sixsteps Songs (BMI), FELLOW SHIPS MUSIC (SESAC), SO ESSENTIAL TUNES (SESAC) and HICKORY BILL DOC (SESAC)
This arrangement © 2022 SOUNDS OF JERICHO (BMI), KRISTIAN STANFILL PUBLISHING DESIGNEE (NS), worshiptogether.com Songs (ASCAP), WORSHIP TOGETHER MUSIC (BMI),
sixsteps Music (ASCAP), sixsteps Songs (BMI), FELLOW SHIPS MUSIC (SESAC), SO ESSENTIAL TUNES (SESAC) and HICKORY BILL DOC (SESAC)
SOUNDS OF JERICHO, KRISTIAN STANFILL PUBLISHING DESIGNEE, worshiptogether.com Songs, WORSHIP TOGETHER MUSIC,
sixsteps Music and sixsteps Songs Admin. at CAPITOLCMGPUBLISHING.COM
FELLOW SHIPS MUSIC, SO ESSENTIAL TUNES and HICKORY BILL DOC Admin. at ESSENTIALMUSICPUBLISHING.COM
All Rights Reserved   Used by Permission

GOOD GOOD FATHER

Words and Music by PAT BARRETT
and ANTHONY BROWN
Arranged by Phillip Keveren

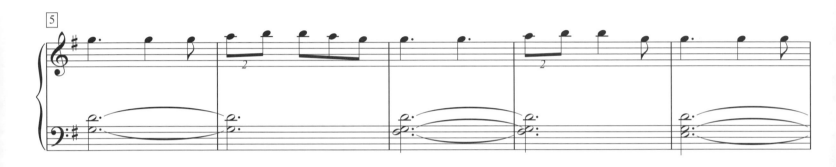

© 2014 COMMON HYMNAL DIGITAL (BMI), HOUSEFIRES SOUNDS (ASCAP), TONY BROWN PUBLISHING DESIGNEE (BMI), worshiptogether.com Songs (ASCAP),
sixsteps Music (ASCAP), VAMOS PUBLISHING (ASCAP) and CAPITOL CMG PARAGON (BMI)
This arrangement © 2022 COMMON HYMNAL DIGITAL (BMI), HOUSEFIRES SOUNDS (ASCAP), TONY BROWN PUBLISHING DESIGNEE (BMI), worshiptogether.com Songs (ASCAP),
sixsteps Music (ASCAP), VAMOS PUBLISHING (ASCAP) and CAPITOL CMG PARAGON (BMI)
Admin. at CAPITOLCMGPUBLISHING.COM
All Rights Reserved   Used by Permission

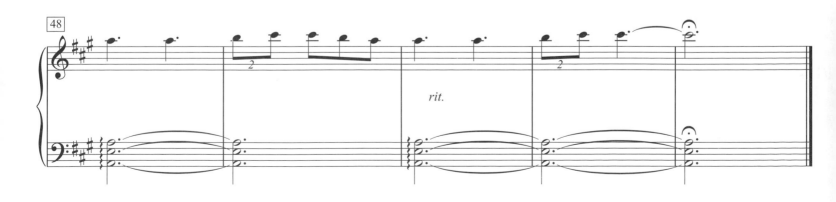

HOLY SPIRIT

Words and Music by KATIE TORWALT
and BRYAN TORWALT
Arranged by Phillip Keveren

With tenderness ♩ = c. 80

© 2011 JESUS CULTURE MUSIC (ASCAP) and CAPITOL CMG GENESIS (ASCAP)
This arrangement © 2022 JESUS CULTURE MUSIC (ASCAP) and CAPITOL CMG GENESIS (ASCAP)
Admin. at CAPITOLCMGPUBLISHING.COM
All Rights Reserved   Used by Permission

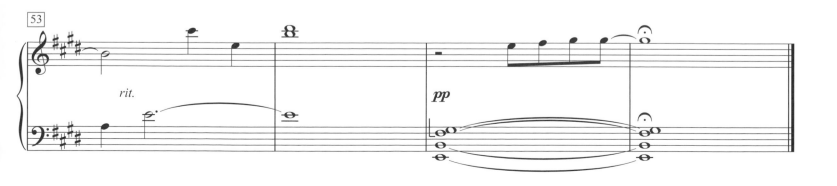

GREAT ARE YOU LORD

Words and Music by JASON INGRAM,
DAVID LEONARD and LESLIE JORDAN
Arranged by Phillip Keveren

Copyright © 2013 Open Hands Music, So Essential Tunes, Integrity's Alleluia! Music and Integrity's Praise! Music
This arrangement Copyright © 2022 Open Hands Music, So Essential Tunes, Integrity's Alleluia! Music and Integrity's Priase! Music
All Rights for Open Hands Music and So Essential Tunes Administered at EssentialMusicPublishing.com
All Rights for Integrity's Alleluia! Music and Integrity's Praise! Music Administered at CapitolCMGPublishing.com
International Copyright Secured   All Rights Reserved

HOW GREAT IS OUR GOD

Words and Music by CHRIS TOMLIN,
JESSE REEVES and ED CASH
Arranged by Phillip Keveren

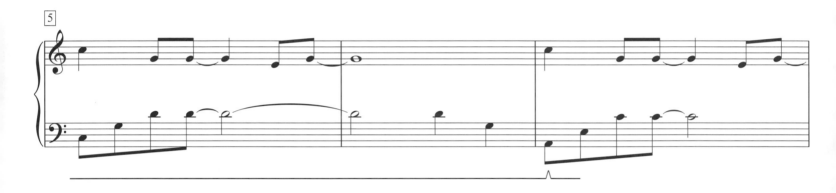

© 2004 worshiptogether.com Songs (ASCAP), sixsteps Music (ASCAP) and WONDROUSLY MADE SONGS (BMI) (a division of Wondrous Worship & Llano Music, LLC)
This arrangement © 2022 worshiptogether.com Songs (ASCAP), sixsteps Music (ASCAP) and WONDROUSLY MADE SONGS (BMI) (a division of Wondrous Worship & Llano Music, LLC)
worshiptogether.com Songs and sixsteps Music Admin. at CAPITOLCMGPUBLISHING.COM
WONDROUSLY MADE SONGS (a division of Wondrous Worship & Llano Music, LLC) Admin. by MUSIC SERVICES
All Rights Reserved   Used by Permission

LIVING HOPE

Words and Music by PHIL WICKHAM
and BRIAN JOHNSON
Arranged by Phillip Keveren

Copyright © 2018 Sing My Songs, Phil Wickham Music, Simply Global Songs and Bethel Music Publishing
This arrangement Copyright © 2022 Sing My Songs, Phil Wickham Music, Simply Global Songs and Bethel Music Publishing
All Rights for Sing My Songs, Phil Wickham Music and Simply Global Songs Admin. at EssentialMusicPublishing.com
All Rights Reserved   Used by Permission

IN CHRIST ALONE

Words and Music by KEITH GETTY
and STUART TOWNEND
Arranged by Phillip Keveren

© 2002 THANKYOU MUSIC (PRS)
This arrangement © 2022 THANKYOU MUSIC (PRS)
Admin. Worldwide at CAPITOLCMGPUBLISHING,.COM excluding Europe which is Admin. by INTEGRITY MUSIC, part of the DAVID C COOK family.
SONGS@INTEGRITYMUSIC.COM
All Rights Reserved   Used by Permission

KING OF MY HEART

Words and Music by JOHN MARK McMILLAN
and SARAH McMILLAN
Arranged by Phillip Keveren

© 2015 MEAUX JEAUX MUSIC (SESAC), RAUCOUS RUCKUS PUBLISHING (SESAC) and WATERSHED MUSIC GROUP (SESAC)
This arrangement © 2022 MEAUX JEAUX MUSIC (SESAC), RAUCOUS RUCKUS PUBLISHING (SESAC) and WATERSHED MUSIC GROUP (SESAC)
MEAUX JEAUX MUSIC and RAUCOUS RUCKUS PUBLISHING Admin. at CAPITOLCMGPUBLISHING.COM
All Rights Reserved   Used by Permission

THE LION AND THE LAMB

Words and Music by BRENTON BROWN,
BRIAN JOHNSON and LEELAND MOORING
Arranged by Phillip Keveren

Reflectively, with freedom ♩ = c. 80

© 2015 THANKYOU MUSIC (PRS), MEAUX MERCY (BMI), THE DEVIL IS A LIAR! PUBLISHING (BMI) and BETHEL MUSIC PUBLISHING (ASCAP)
This arrangement © 2022 THANKYOU MUSIC (PRS), MEAUX MERCY (BMI), THE DEVIL IS A LIAR! PUBLISHING (BMI) and BETHEL MUSIC PUBLISHING (ASCAP)
THANKYOU MUSIC Admin. Worldwide at CAPITOLCMGPUBLISHING.COM excluding Europe which is Admin. by INTEGRITY MUSIC, part of the DAVID C COOK family.
SONGS@INTEGRITYMUSIC.COM
MEAUX MERCY and THE DEVIL IS A LIAR! PUBLISHING Admin. at CAPITOLCMGPUBLISHING.COM
All Rights Reserved   Used by Permission

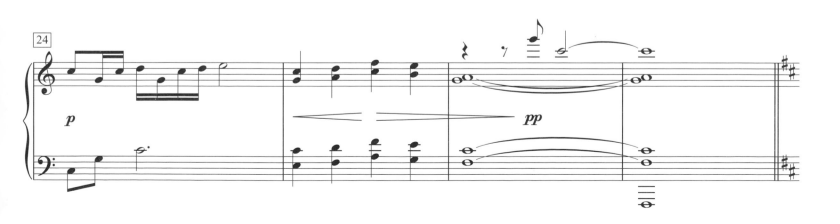

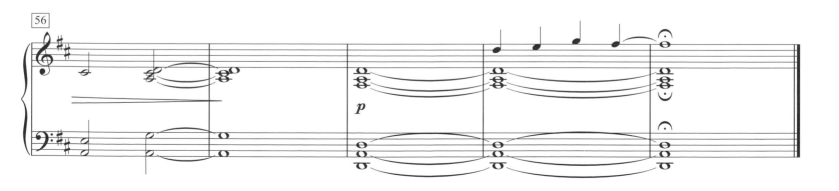

LORD, I NEED YOU

Words and Music by JESSE REEVES,
KRISTIAN STANFILL, MATT MAHER,
CHRISTY NOCKELS and DANIEL CARSON
Arranged by Phillip Keveren

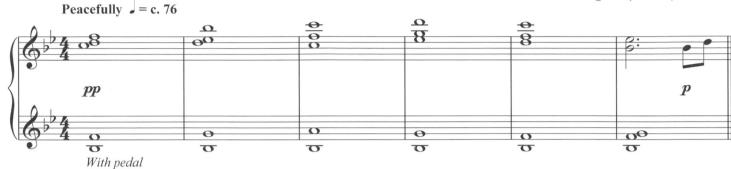

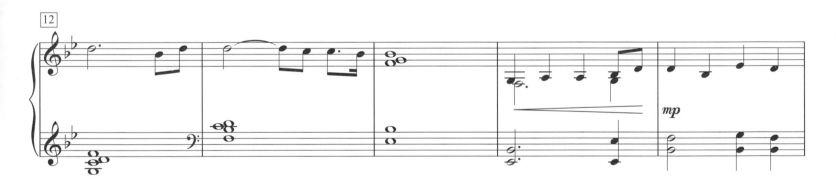

© 2011 THANKYOU MUSIC (PRS), worshiptogether.com Songs (ASCAP), sixsteps Music (ASCAP), SWEATER WEATHER MUSIC (ASCAP) and VALLEY OF SONGS MUSIC (BMI)
This arrangement © 2022 THANKYOU MUSIC (PRS), worshiptogether.com Songs (ASCAP), sixsteps Music (ASCAP),
SWEATER WEATHER MUSIC (ASCAP) and VALLEY OF SONGS MUSIC (BMI)
THANKYOU MUSIC Admin. Worldwide at CAPITOLCMGPUBLISHING.COM excluding Europe which is Admin. by INTEGRITY MUSIC, a part of the DAVID C COOK family.
SONGS@INTEGRITYMUSIC.COM
worshiptogether.com Songs, sixsteps Music, SWEATER WEATHER MUSIC and VALLEY OF SONGS MUSIC Admin. at CAPITOLCMGPUBLISHING.COM
All Rights Reserved   Used by Permission

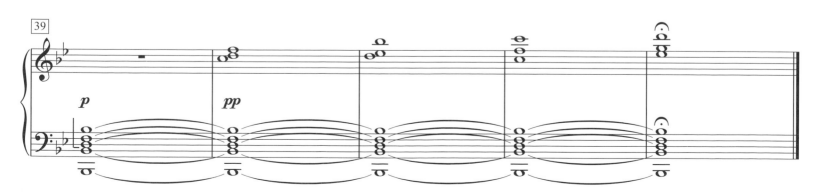

O COME TO THE ALTAR

Words and Music by CHRIS BROWN,
MACK BROCK, STEVEN FURTICK
and WADE JOYE
Arranged by Phillip Keveren

Copyright © 2016 Music By Elevation Worship Publishing
This arrangement Copyright © 2022 Music By Elevation Worship Publishing
All Rights Administered at EssentialMusicPublishing.com
All Rights Reserved   Used by Permission

O PRAISE THE NAME
(Anastasis)

Words and Music by MARTY SAMPSON,
BENJAMIN HASTINGS and DEAN USSHER
Arranged by Phillip Keveren

With reverence ♩= c. 72

With pedal

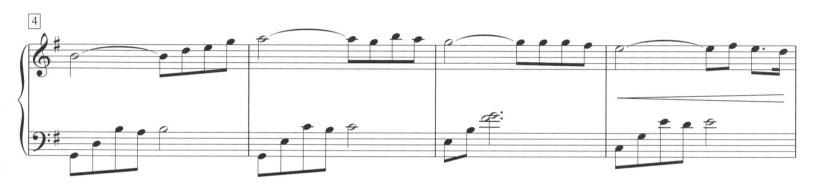

© 2015 HILLSONG MUSIC PUBLISHING (APRA)
This arrangement © 2022 HILLSONG MUSIC PUBLISHING (APRA)
Admin. in the United States and Canada at CAPITOLCMGPUBLISHING.COM
All Rights Reserved   Used by Permission

RECKLESS LOVE

Words and Music by CALEB CULVER,
CORY ASBURY and RAN JACKSON
Arranged by Phillip Keveren

Copyright © 2017, 2018 Bethel Music Publishing (ASCAP), Watershed Publishing Group (ASCAP) and Richmond Park Publishing (BMI)
This arrangement Copyright © 2022 Bethel Music Publishing (ASCAP), Watershed Publishing Group (ASCAP) and Richmond Park Publishing (BMI)
All Rights for Richmond Park Publishing Admin. at EssentialMusicPublishing.com
All Rights Reserved   Used by Permission

10,000 REASONS
(Bless the Lord)

Words and Music by JONAS MYRIN
and MATT REDMAN
Arranged by Phillip Keveren

Slowly, with rubato throughout ♩ = c. 66

© 2011 ATLAS MOUNTAIN SONGS (BMI), worshiptogether.com Songs (ASCAP), sixsteps Music (ASCAP) and THANKYOU MUSIC (PRS)
This arrangement © 2022 ATLAS MOUNTAIN SONGS (BMI), worshiptogether.com Songs (ASCAP), sixsteps Music (ASCAP) and THANKYOU MUSIC (PRS)
ATLAS MOUNTAIN SONGS, worshiptogether.com Songs and sixsteps Music Admin. at CAPITOLCMGPUBLISHING.COM
THANKYOU MUSIC Admin. Worldwide at CAPITOLCMGPUBLISHING,.COM excluding Europe which is Admin. by INTEGRITY MUSIC, part of the DAVID C COOK family.
SONGS@INTEGRITYMUSIC.COM
All Rights Reserved   Used by Permission

THIS IS AMAZING GRACE

Words and Music by PHIL WICKHAM,
JOSHUA NEIL FARRO and JEREMY RIDDLE
Arranged by Phillip Keveren

© 2012 SING MY SONGS (BMI), SEEMS LIKE MUSIC (BMI), PHIL WICKHAM MUSIC (BMI), WC MUSIC CORP. (ASCAP),
JOSH'S MUSIC (ASCAP), FBR MUSIC (ASCAP) and BETHEL MUSIC PUBLISHING (ASCAP)
This arrangement © 2022 SING MY SONGS (BMI), SEEMS LIKE MUSIC (BMI), PHIL WICKHAM MUSIC (BMI), WC MUSIC CORP. (ASCAP),
JOSH'S MUSIC (ASCAP), FBR MUSIC (ASCAP) and BETHEL MUSIC PUBLISHING (ASCAP)
SING MY SONGS, SEEMS LIKE MUSIC and PHIL WICKHAM MUSIC Administered by BMG RIGHTS MANAGEMENT c/o MUSIC SERVICES
JOSH'S MUSIC and FBR MUSIC Administered by WC MUSIC CORP.
All Rights Reserved   Used by Permission

WHAT A BEAUTIFUL NAME

Words and Music by BEN FIELDING
and BROOKE LIGERTWOOD
Arranged by Phillip Keveren

Serenely, with rubato ♩ = c. 60

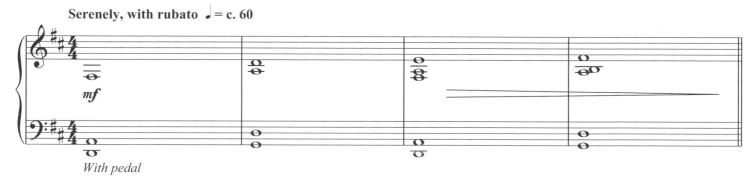

© 2016 HILLSONG MUSIC PUBLISHING (APRA)
This arrangement © 2022 HILLSONG MUSIC PUBLISHING (APRA)
Admin. in the United States and Canada at CAPITOLCMGPUBLISHING.COM
All Rights Reserved   Used by Permission

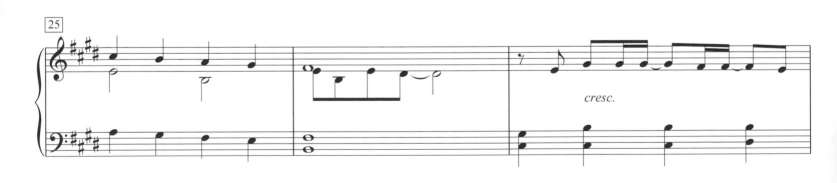

WHO YOU SAY I AM

Words and Music by REUBEN MORGAN
and BEN FIELDING
Arranged by Phillip Keveren

© 2018 HILLSONG MUSIC PUBLISHING (APRA)
This arrangement © 2022 HILLSONG MUSIC PUBLISHING (APRA)
Admin. in the United States and Canada at CAPITOLCMGPUBLISHING.COM
All Rights Reserved   Used by Permission

THE PHILLIP KEVEREN SERIES

PIANO SOLO

00156644	ABBA for Classical Piano	$15.99
00311024	Above All	$12.99
00311348	Americana	$12.99
00198473	Bach Meets Jazz	$14.99
00313594	Bacharach and David	$15.99
00306412	The Beatles	$19.99
00312189	The Beatles for Classical Piano	$17.99
00275876	The Beatles – Recital Suites	$19.99
00312546	Best Piano Solos	$15.99
00156601	Blessings	$14.99
00198656	Blues Classics	$14.99
00284359	Broadway Songs with a Classical Flair	$14.99
00310669	Broadway's Best	$16.99
00312106	Canzone Italiana	$12.99
00280848	Carpenters	$17.99
00310629	A Celtic Christmas	$14.99
00310549	The Celtic Collection	$14.99
00280571	Celtic Songs with a Classical Flair	$12.99
00263362	Charlie Brown Favorites	$14.99
00312190	Christmas at the Movies	$15.99
00294754	Christmas Carols with a Classical Flair	$12.99
00311414	Christmas Medleys	$14.99
00236669	Christmas Praise Hymns	$12.99
00233788	Christmas Songs for Classical Piano	$14.99
00311769	Christmas Worship Medleys	$14.99
00310607	Cinema Classics	$15.99
00301857	Circles	$10.99
00311101	Classic Wedding Songs	$12.99
00311292	Classical Folk	$10.95
00311083	Classical Jazz	$14.99
00137779	Coldplay for Classical Piano	$16.99
00311103	Contemporary Wedding Songs	$12.99
00348788	Country Songs with a Classical Flair	$14.99
00249097	Disney Recital Suites	$17.99
00311754	Disney Songs for Classical Piano	$17.99
00241379	Disney Songs for Ragtime Piano	$17.99
00364812	The Essential Hymn Anthology	$34.99
00311881	Favorite Wedding Songs	$14.99
00315974	Fiddlin' at the Piano	$12.99
00311811	The Film Score Collection	$15.99
00269408	Folksongs with a Classical Flair	$12.99
00144353	The Gershwin Collection	$14.99
00233789	Golden Scores	$14.99
00144351	Gospel Greats	$14.99
00183566	The Great American Songbook	$14.99
00312084	The Great Melodies	$14.99
00311157	Great Standards	$14.99
00171621	A Grown-Up Christmas List	$14.99
00311071	The Hymn Collection	$14.99
00311349	Hymn Medleys	$14.99
00280705	Hymns in a Celtic Style	$14.99

00269407	Hymns with a Classical Flair	$14.99
00311249	Hymns with a Touch of Jazz	$14.99
00310905	I Could Sing of Your Love Forever	$16.99
00310762	Jingle Jazz	$15.99
00175310	Billy Joel for Classical Piano	$16.99
00126449	Elton John for Classical Piano	$19.99
00310839	Let Freedom Ring!	$12.99
00238988	Andrew Lloyd Webber Piano Songbook	$14.99
00313227	Andrew Lloyd Webber Solos	$17.99
00313523	Mancini Magic	$16.99
00312113	More Disney Songs for Classical Piano	$16.99
00311295	Motown Hits	$14.99
00300640	Piano Calm	$12.99
00339131	Piano Calm: Christmas	$14.99
00346009	Piano Calm: Prayer	$14.99
00306870	Piazzolla Tangos	$17.99
00386709	Praise and Worship for Classical Piano	$14.99
00156645	Queen for Classical Piano	$17.99
00310755	Richard Rodgers Classics	$17.99
00289545	Scottish Songs	$12.99
00119403	The Sound of Music	$16.99
00311978	The Spirituals Collection	$12.99
00366023	So Far...	$14.99
00210445	Star Wars	$16.99
00224738	Symphonic Hymns for Piano	$14.99
00366022	Three-Minute Encores	$16.99
00279673	Tin Pan Alley	$12.99
00312112	Treasured Hymns for Classical Piano	$15.99
00144926	The Twelve Keys of Christmas	$14.99
00278486	The Who for Classical Piano	$16.99
00294036	Worship with a Touch of Jazz	$14.99
00311911	Yuletide Jazz	$19.99

EASY PIANO

00210401	Adele for Easy Classical Piano	$17.99
00310610	African-American Spirituals	$12.99
00218244	The Beatles for Easy Classical Piano	$14.99
00218387	Catchy Songs for Piano	$12.99
00310973	Celtic Dreams	$12.99
00233686	Christmas Carols for Easy Classical Piano	$14.99
00311126	Christmas Pops	$16.99
00368199	Christmas Reflections	$14.99
00311548	Classic Pop/Rock Hits	$14.99
00310769	A Classical Christmas	$14.99
00310975	Classical Movie Themes	$12.99
00144352	Disney Songs for Easy Classical Piano	$14.99
00311093	Early Rock 'n' Roll	$14.99
00311997	Easy Worship Medleys	$14.99
00289547	Duke Ellington	$14.99
00160297	Folksongs for Easy Classical Piano	$12.99

00110374	George Gershwin Classics	$14.99
00310805	Gospel Treasures	$14.99
00306821	Vince Guaraldi Collection	$19.99
00160294	Hymns for Easy Classical Piano	$14.99
00310798	Immortal Hymns	$12.99
00311294	Jazz Standards	$12.99
00355474	Living Hope	$14.99
00310744	Love Songs	$14.99
00233740	The Most Beautiful Songs for Easy Classical Piano	$12.99
00220036	Pop Ballads	$14.99
00311406	Pop Gems of the 1950s	$12.95
00233739	Pop Standards for Easy Classical Piano	$12.99
00102887	A Ragtime Christmas	$12.99
00311293	Ragtime Classics	$14.99
00312028	Santa Swings	$14.99
00233688	Songs from Childhood for Easy Classical Piano	$12.99
00103258	Songs of Inspiration	$14.99
00310840	Sweet Land of Liberty	$12.99
00126450	10,000 Reasons	$16.99
00310712	Timeless Praise	$14.99
00311086	TV Themes	$14.99
00310717	21 Great Classics	$14.99
00160076	Waltzes & Polkas for Easy Classical Piano	$12.99
00145342	Weekly Worship	$17.99

BIG-NOTE PIANO

00310838	Children's Favorite Movie Songs	$14.99
00346000	Christmas Movie Magic	$12.99
00277368	Classical Favorites	$12.99
00277370	Disney Favorites	$14.99
00310888	Joy to the World	$12.99
00310908	The Nutcracker	$12.99
00277371	Star Wars	$16.99

BEGINNING PIANO SOLOS

00311202	Awesome God	$14.99
00310837	Christian Children's Favorites	$14.99
00311117	Christmas Traditions	$10.99
00311250	Easy Hymns	$12.99
00102710	Everlasting God	$10.99
00311403	Jazzy Tunes	$10.95
00310822	Kids' Favorites	$12.99
00367778	A Magical Christmas	$14.99
00338175	Silly Songs for Kids	$9.99

PIANO DUET

00126452	The Christmas Variations	$14.99
00362562	Classic Piano Duets	$14.99
00311350	Classical Theme Duets	$12.99
00295099	Gospel Duets	$12.99
00311544	Hymn Duets	$14.99
00311203	Praise & Worship Duets	$14.99
00294755	Sacred Christmas Duets	$14.99
00119405	Star Wars	$16.99
00253545	Worship Songs for Two	$12.99

Search songlists, more products and place your order from your favorite music retailer at
halleonard.com

Disney characters and artwork
TM & © 2021 Disney LLC

Prices, contents, and availability subject to change without notice.

0422
158

ALSO AVAILABLE

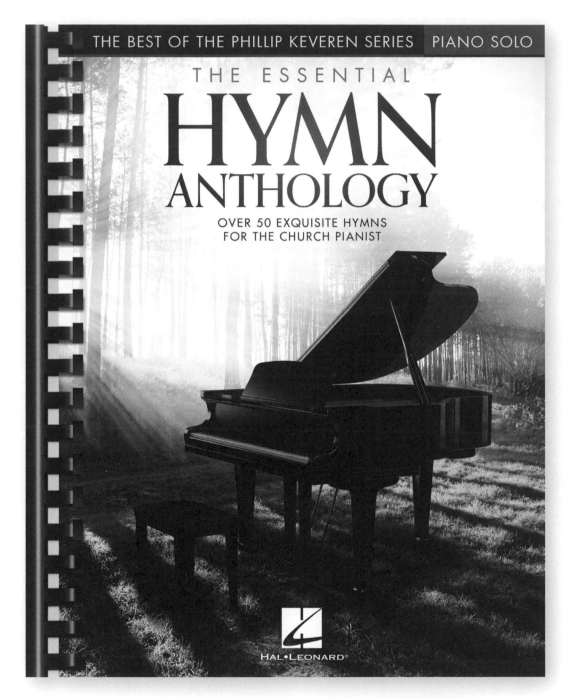

HL 364812 THE ESSENTIAL HYMN ANTHOLOGY
Church pianists will treasure this beautiful comb-bound
collection, the first in the Best of Phillip Keveren Series.